AAT

Financial Statements of Limited Companies

Pocket Notes

These Pocket Notes support study for the following AAT qualifications:

AAT Professional Diploma in Accounting – Level 4

AAT Level 4 Diploma in Business Skills

AAT Professional Diploma in Accounting at SCQF Level 8

Certificate: Accounting (Level 5 AATSA)

KAPLAN

PUBLISHING

British library cataloguing-in-publication data

A catalogue record for this book is available from the British Library.

Published by:
Kaplan Publishing UK
Unit 2 The Business Centre
Molly Millars Lane
Wokingham
Berkshire
RG41 2QZ

ISBN 978-1-78415-611-4

© Kaplan Financial Limited, 2016

Printed and bound in Great Britain.

CONTENTS

Preface

These Pocket Notes contain the key things that you need to know for the exam, presented in a unique visual way that makes revision easy and effective.

Written by experienced lecturers and authors, these Pocket Notes break down content into manageable chunks to maximise your concentration.

Quality and accuracy are of the utmost importance to us so if you spot an error in any of our products, please send an email to mykaplanreporting@kaplan.com with full details, or follow the link to the feedback form in MyKaplan.

Our Quality Co-ordinator will work with our technical team to verify the error and take action to ensure it is corrected in future editions.

A guide to the assessment

- Note on the conceptual framework.
- Examinable International Financial Reporting Standards (both IFRS and IAS).

The assessment

This unit is concerned with competence in drafting and interpreting the financial statements of limited companies.

Learners will have already attained competence at Levels 2 and 3 in the process of identifying and recording financial transactions in accounts and ledgers following the principles of double entry bookkeeping. They will already be able to draft the financial statements of sole traders and partnerships. This unit develops and applies these competencies further by focusing on the drafting and interpretation of financial statements of limited companies.

Learners are also introduced to tools and techniques that can be used to analyse and interpret the financial performance and financial position of a company.

Examination

Financial Statements of Limited Companies (FSLC) is assessed by means of a computer based assessment (CBA). The CBA will last for two and a half hours and will consist of 8 tasks.

In any one assessment, learners may not be assessed on all content, or on the full depth or breadth of a piece of content. The content assessed may change over time to ensure validity of assessment, but all assessment criteria will be assessed over time.

Learning outcomes and weighting

1. Demonstrate an understanding of the reporting frameworks and ethical principles that underpin financial reporting   7%

2. Demonstrate an understanding of the key features of a published set of financial statements   18%

3. Draft statutory financial statements for a limited company   27%

4. Draft consolidated financial statements   20%

5. Interpret financial statements using ratio analysis   28%

Total   100%

Pass mark

To pass a unit assessment, students need to achieve a mark of 70% or more.

This unit contributes 15% of the total amount required for the Professional Diploma in Accounting qualification.

Note on the Conceptual Framework

The Conceptual Framework for Financial Reporting 2010 identifies one assumption underlying the preparation of financial statements – the going concern assumption. However, the AAT have confirmed that the unit specification for Financial Statements of Limited Companies departs from this and states that there are two underlying assumptions; going concern and the accruals basis.

Examinable International Financial Reporting Standards (both IFRS and IAS)

IAS 1   Presentation of Financial Statements

IAS 2   Inventories

IAS 7   Statement of Cash Flows

IAS 10   Events After the Reporting Period

IAS 12   Income Taxes

IAS 16   Property, Plant and Equipment

IAS 17   Leases

IAS 18   Revenue

IAS 36   Impairment of Assets

IAS 37   Provisions, Contingent Liabilities and Contingent Assets

IAS 38   Intangible Assets

IFRS 3   Business Combinations

IFRS 10   Consolidated Financial Statements

Additional reading

A student's guide to International Financial Reporting Standards by Clare Finch

ISBN 978 1 84710 708 4

1

The reporting frameworks and ethical principles

- Overview.
- IFRS foundation.
- Legal framework.
- IASB framework.
- IAS 1 Presentation of Financial Statements.
- The fundamental ethical principles of the AAT Code of Professional Ethics.
  - The threats.
  - Safeguards.

Overview

This chapter gives information on:

- the regulatory environment (company law and the IFRS Foundation)
- the conceptual framework (the Conceptual Framework for Financial Reporting).

CBA focus

You may be required to discuss or explain topics in this chapter as part of an examination task.

IFRS foundation

The structure of the International Financial Reporting Standards Foundation (IFRS Foundation) and its subsidiary bodies is shown below:

Key Point

- The IFRS Foundation is an independent not for profit foundation based in the US whose trustees appoint the members of the IASB, IFRS AC and IFRS IC.

- The IASB is responsible for developing and issuing new accounting standards. The IASB issues International Financial Reporting Standards (IFRSs) and has adopted the previous International Accounting Standards (IASs).

- The IFRS AC advises the IASB on priorities in its work and informs the IASB of the implications of proposed standards for users and preparers of financial statements.

- The IFRS IC draws up interpretations if a new problem arises or gives guidance on the application of a standard where unsatisfactory interpretations exist.

Legal framework

- In the UK, companies must prepare their financial statements following the rules laid out in the Companies Act 2006 (CA06).

- The CA06 has been amended to reflect the fact that some companies prepare their financial statements based upon the application of IFRSs.

- In the UK, the Financial Reporting Council (FRC) prepares accounting standards. In recent years there has been a process of harmonisation between UK and International standards and the majority of UK standards are now equivalent to IFRSs.

IASB framework

The IASB's Conceptual Framework for Financial Reporting identifies the principles on which accounting standards are to be developed. It aims to assist in the preparation of financial statements, development of new standards and to reduce alternative accounting treatments.

Key Point

- The underlying assumption of financial statements is that they are prepared on a going concern basis.

- There are two fundamental qualitative characteristics together with four enhancing characteristics:

The two fundamental qualitative characteristics:

- **Relevance** – financial information is regarded as relevant if it capable of influencing the decision of users.

- **Faithful representation** – this means that financial information must be complete, neutral and free from error.

The four enhancing qualititative characteristics:

- **Comparability** – it should be possible to compare an entity over time and with similar information about other entities.

- **Verifiability** – if information can be verified (e.g. through an audit) this provides assurance to the users that it is both credible and reliable.

- **Timeliness** – information should be provided to users within a timescale suitable for their decision making purposes.

- **Understandability** – information should be understandable to those that might want to review and use it. This can be facilitated through appropriate classification, characterisation and presentation of information.

Elements of the financial statements

Asset: a resource controlled by an entity as a result of past events and from which future economic benefits are expected to flow to the entity.

Liability: a present obligation of the entity arising from past events, the settlement of which is expected to result in an outflow from the enterprise of resources embodying economic benefits.

Equity: the residual interest in the assets of the entity after deducting all its liabilities.

Income: income consists of both revenue and gains. Revenue arises from a business's ordinary activities such as the sale of goods. Gains represent increases in economic benefits such as a gain on disposal of a non-current asset and are not normally shown within revenue.

Expenses: expenses are losses as well as expenses that arise in the normal course of business such as cost of sales, wages and depreciation. Losses represent a decrease in economic benefits such as losses on disposal of non-current assets or disasters such as fire or flood and are often shown separately in the financial statements.

Recognition of items in the financial statements

Recognition of (i.e. recording) an item in the financial statements occurs if:

- the item meets the definition of an element
- it is probable that any future economic benefit associated with the item will flow to or from the entity
- it can be measured at a monetary amount with sufficient reliability.

IAS 1 Presentation of Financial Statements

IAS 1 provides formats for the statement of profit or loss, statement of financial position and statement of changes in equity as well as setting out six accounting concepts that should be applied:

- **going concern** – the business will continue in operation for the foreseeable future
- **accruals** – the effects of transactions and other events are recognised as they occur and not as cash or its equivalent is received or paid
- **consistency of presentation** – items in the financial statements are presented and classified in the same way from one period to the next unless there is a change in the operations of the business or a new standard requires a change in presentation

- **materiality and aggregation** – each material class of similar items shall be presented separately in the financial statements
- **offsetting** – assets and liabilities and income and expenses cannot be offset unless a standard requires it
- **comparative information** – should be shown for all amounts reported in the financial statements.

Accounting policies should be selected so that the financial statements comply with all international standards and interpretations.

An entity must make an explicit statement in the notes to the financial statements that they comply with IFRS.

The fundamental principles of the AAT Code of Professional Ethics

Outlined below are the key principles of the AAT Code of Professional Ethics;

Professional competence and due care

A professional accountant has a continuing duty to maintain professional knowledge and skill at the level required to ensure that a client or employer receives competent professional service based on current developments in practice, legislation and techniques.

Objectivity

A professional accountant should not allow bias, conflict of interest or undue influence of others to override professional or business judgements.

Confidentiality

A professional accountant should respect the confidentiality of information acquired as a result of professional and business relationships and should not disclose any such information to third parties without proper and specific authority unless there is a legal or professional right or duty to disclose.

Professional behaviour

A person should not act in any way that is unprofessional or does not comply with relevant laws and regulations.

Integrity

A person should be straightforward and honest in performing professional work and in all business relationships.

The threats

The following are all examples of behaviour that could threaten an accountant's objectivity or independence from their clients:

The self-interest threat – may occur because of a financial or other interest held by the accountant or a family member.

The advocacy threat – may occur when an accountant is asked to promote or represent their client in some way. In this situation the accountant would have to be biased in favour of the client and therefore cannot be objective.

The self-review threat – when work you have previously prepared needs review – you cannot audit your own work.

The familiarity or trust threat – this occurs when the accountant is too sympathetic or trusting of the client because of a close relationship with them.

The intimidation threat – may occur when an accountant may be deterred from acting objectively by threats – actual or perceived.

Safeguards

Safeguards are controls to reduce or eliminate threats. They fall into two broad categories:

(i) Safeguards created by the profession, legislation or regulation. Examples of these include:

- Educational, training and experience requirements for entry into the profession.
- Continuing professional development requirements.
- Corporate governance regulations.
- Professional standards.

- External review by a legally empowered third party of the reports, returns, communications or information produced by a professional accountant.

(ii) Safeguards in the work environment. Examples of these include:

- Policies and procedures to implement and monitor quality control of engagements.

- A disciplinary procedure to promote compliance with policies and procedures.

- Policies and procedures to monitor and, if necessary, manage the reliance on revenue received from a single client.

2

Limited company financial statements

- Overview.
- Features of limited companies.
- Contents of company financial statements.
- Company finance.
- Share issues.
- Dividends.
- Tax.

Overview

- The chapter explains the main 'legal' features of limited liability companies which distinguish them from sole traders and partnerships.

- The information and statements making up the financial statements of a company are introduced, with particular emphasis on the 'Statement of changes in equity' – this statement is relevant only to companies.

- The main sources of company finance (equity and debt) are introduced together with an explanation of the items which may be encountered under each of these headings.

- The accounting treatment of the following are explained:

  - Share issues, including bonus and rights issues.

  - Dividends.

  - Taxation.

Features of limited companies

Companies are distinguished from other types of business by the following three factors:

1. The law regards a company as a **separate legal entity** from its shareholders.

2. The **separation of the ownership** (shareholders) **from the management** (directors) of the company.

3. The **limited liability** of shareholders for the debts of a company. Their liability is limited to any portion of the nominal value of shares that is unpaid.

Key points:

- The shareholders can share in the profits of the company without having to work in the business on a day-to-day basis.
- It is easy for a company to borrow money, as they are able to as they are able to raise loan finance by the issue of a debenture.
- If the shareholders die the company will not cease trading which would be the case with a sole trader.
- Companies may have to be audited and have to prepare their financial statements according to prescribed formats.
- There is more administration to deal with in a company such as filing financial statements with the Registrar of Companies.
- Companies are regulated by the Companies Act 2006 and accounting standards issued by the IASB.

Contents of company financial statements

A set of financial statements includes the following statements:

Statement of financial position	**Statement of profit or loss**
Statement of changes in equity	**Statement of cash flows**

The other parts of the financial statements are:

- **Accounting policy note** – to disclose the policies adopted by the company for items in the financial statements.
- **Notes to the financial statements** – to provide more detailed information about the figures included in the statement of financial position, statement of profit or loss and statement of cash flows.

- **Comparative figures** – to show the position in the previous financial year for comparison purposes.

Formats

The format of the statement of profit or loss and other comprehensive income is detailed in IAS 1 Presentation of Financial Statements and is shown below.

Statement of profit or loss and other comprehensive income	**£**
Continuing operations	
Revenue	X
Cost of sales	(X)
Gross profit	X
Distribution costs	(X)
Administrative expenses	(X)
Profit from operations	X
Finance costs	(X)
Profit before tax	X
Tax	(X)
Profit for the period from continuing operations	X
Other comprehensive income for the year	
Gain on revaluation of land	X
Total comprehensive income for year	X

The statement of financial position and principal notes to the accounts are shown below.

Company statement of financial position at 31 December 20XX

ASSETS	£000
Non-current assets	
Goodwill	X
Other intangible assets	X
Property, plant and equipment	X
Investments in subsidiaries	X
Investments in associates	X
Current assets	
Inventories	X
Trade and other receivables	X
Cash and cash equivalents	X
Total assets	X

EQUITY AND LIABILITIES

Equity

Share capital	X
Share premium account	X
Revaluation surplus	X
Retained earnings	X
Total equity	**X**

Non-current liabilities

Bank loans	X
Long-term provisions	X

Current liabilities

Trade and other payables	X
Tax liabilities	X
Bank overdrafts and loans	X
Total equity and liabilities	**X**

An example of a property, plant and equipment note is shown below:

	Land and buildings	Plant and machinery	Fixtures, fittings, and equipment	Total
	£000	£000	£000	£000
Cost or valuation:				
At 1 January 20XX	X	X	X	X
Additions	X	X	X	X
Disposals	–	(X)	(X)	(X)
At 31 December 20XX	X	X	X	X

Continued on next page:-

	Land and buildings	Plant and machinery	Fixtures, fittings, tools and equipment	Total
	£000	£000	£000	£000
Accumulated depreciation:				
At 1 January 20XX	X	X	X	X
Charge for year	X	X	X	X
Disposals	–	(X)	(X)	(X)
At 31 December 20XX	X	X	X	X
Carrying amount:				
at 1 January 20XX	X	X	X	X
at 31 December 20XX	X	X	X	X

Statement of Changes in Equity

Below is a pro forma Statement of Changes in Equity:

	Share capital £000	Share premium £000	Revaluation surplus £000	Retained earnings £000	Total £000
At 1 January 20XX	X	X	X	X	X
Total comprehensive income for the year			X	X	X
Dividends paid				(X)	(X)
At 31 December 20XX	X	X	X	X	X

Key points:

The statement of changes in equity:

- This statement shows all the gains and losses in the period including those which are not recognised in the statement of profit or loss such as revaluation surpluses.
- As the statement of profit or loss does not show dividends paid in the period, this is also shown in this statement.
- It is essentially a reconciliation of share capital and reserves from the opening to the closing position.

Company finance

The way companies are financed varies from one company to another. Typically, companies will have a combination of equity finance (from shareholders) and debt finance (from banks and other lenders).

Company finance

Equity
- Ordinary shares
- Preference shares

Debt
- Bank overdraft
- Trade payables
- Debentures or loan stock

- **Ordinary shares** (or equity shares) give shareholders the right to vote at general meetings of the company and to receive dividends from profits.

- **Preference shares** carry a fixed rate of dividend but the shareholders are not given a vote. The preference dividend is paid in priority to the ordinary dividend.

- **Debentures or loan stock** are loans shown as liabilities in the statement of financial position. A debenture may be a loan from one person, whereas loan stock may be held by a number of individuals, like shares.

- These loans have interest charged which is an expense in the statement of profit or loss. The accounting entries are:

  DR Interest expense

      CR Accruals/cash (depending on whether the cash has actually been paid).

Share issues

Shares may be issued at their nominal (or par) value or at a premium (an amount in excess of their nominal value).

Example

A Ltd issued 1,000 ordinary shares with a nominal value of £1 for £1.20 cash.

The double entry to record this is:

	£	£
DR Cash (1,000 × £1.20)	1,200	
CR Share capital (nominal value = 1,000 × £1)		1,000
CR Share premium (1,000 × £0.2)		200

Bonus issues

Extra shares are issued to existing shareholders in proportion to their shareholding without any money being paid for them.

The accounting entries are:

DR   Retained earnings (or any other reserve, such as revaluation surplus or share premium)

CR   Share capital

This may be done to increase the number of shares so that the share price is reduced and the shares are more marketable.

Rights issues

Extra shares are issued at a favourable price to existing shareholders. The number of shares they can buy is in proportion to their existing shareholding, such as 1 share for every 5 they own – a 1 for 5 issue.

The accounting entries are the same as a normal share issue.

Example

A Ltd has 400,000 50p ordinary shares in issue and makes a rights issue of 100,000 50p ordinary shares at 90p per share. The issue is fully taken up.

Required:
Show the entries in the relevant ledger accounts.

Tutorial note
Rights issue: 100,000 x £0.50 = £50,000 is entered in the share capital account. 100,000 x £0.40 = £40,000 is entered in the share premium account.

Solution

Share capital

	£		£
Balance c/d	250,000	Balance b/f (400,000 x 0.5)	200,000
		Bank (100,000 x 0.5)	50,000
	250,000		250,000
		Balance b/d	250,000

Bank

	£		£
Share capital	50,000		
Share premium	40,000		
	90,000		

Share premium

	£		£
Balance c/d	40,000	Bank (100,000 x 0.4)	40,000
	40,000		40,000
		Balance b/d	40,000

Dividends

- Dividends are payments made to shareholders. They can be stated as an amount per share e.g. 5c per share dividend or on a percentage basis e.g. 5% on a £1 share.

- Both the interim and final dividends paid are shown in the notes to the financial statements. Any dividends declared before the year end are included in payables. The double entry bookkeeping for dividends is as follows:

Interim dividend paid:

Dr Retained Earnings

Cr Cash

Final dividend payable:

Dr Retained Earnings

Cr Payables

Tax

- Companies must pay tax on their profits.
- At the year-end, the tax is estimated and charged in the statement of profit or loss.
- In the UK corporation tax is paid nine months after the year-end so the amount provided might not be the actual amount paid.
- When the tax is estimated, the accounting entries are:

  DR Tax expense (P/L)
      CR Tax payable. (SFP)

- When the tax is paid, the accounting entries are:

  DR Tax payable (SFP)
      CR Cash. (SFP)

- Any under or overprovision of tax must be adjusted in the following year's financial statements.

- If the company provided for too much tax then there will be a credit in the following year's tax charge.
- If the company didn't provide enough tax then the following year will have an additional charge of the shortfall.

For the year ended 30 September 20X7, the estimated tax charge was £30,000.

For the year ended 30 September 20X8, the estimated tax charge was £40,000, and the actual tax paid for the previous year was £32,000.

Show these entries in the tax expense accounts for the two years.

Solution

Taxation expense

	£		£
20X7			
Tax liability a/c	30,000	Profit or loss	30,000
	30,000		30,000
20X8			
Tax Liability a/c (underprovision 20X7)	2,000	Profit or loss	42,000
Tax liability a/c	40,000		
	42,000		42,000

3

Statement of cash flows

- Overview.
- Preparing a statement of cash flows.
- Interpretation of a statement of cash flows.

Overview

This chapter deals with:

- The purpose of a statement of cash flows and the information which it provides in addition to that contained in the statement of financial position and statement of profit or loss.

- The suggested format of a statement of cash flows in accordance with IAS 7 is presented and explained.

- The technique for the preparation of a statement of cash flows in an examination is illustrated.

- The points to look for when interpreting a statement of cash flows are outlined.

CBA focus

It is very likely that part of a task in your examination may involve the preparation of a statement of cash flows.

- A statement of cash flows can provide information on a company's liquidity, viability and adaptability.

- It may assist users of financial statements in making judgements on the amount, timing and degree of certainty of future cash flows.

- It gives an indication of the relationship between profitability and cash generating ability, and thus of the quality of the profit earned.

CBA focus

The examination may divide the statement into two parts.

- 'Profit before tax' to 'Net cash from operating activities'; and

- 'Net cash from operating activities' to 'cash and cash equivalents at the end of period'.

IAS 7 Statement of Cash Flows does not prescribe a strict format for the statement of cash flow, but it requires that it is split into three sections – operating, investing and financing.

XYZ Ltd, Statement of cash flows for the year ended 31 December 20X7

	£000	£000
Cash flows from operating activities		
Profit from operations	X	
Adjustments for:		
Depreciation charges	X	
Loss/(Profit) on sale of non-current asset	X/(X)	
	X	
(Increase)/decrease in inventories	(X)/X	
(Increase)/decrease in trade and other receivables	(X)/X	
Increase/(decrease) in trade payables	X/(X)	
Cash generated from operations	X	
Interest paid	(X)	
Tax paid	(X)	
Net cash from operating activities		X
Cash flows from investing activities		
Cash paid to purchase property, plant and equipment	(X)	
Cash proceeds from sale of PPE	X	
Interest received	X	
Dividends received	X	
Net cash used in investing activities		(X)
Cash flows from financing activities		
Proceeds from issue of shares	X	
Redemption of long term borrowing	(X)	
Dividends paid	(X)	
Net cash used in financing activities		(X)
Net increase in cash and cash equivalents		X
Cash and cash equivalents at beginning of period		X
Cash and cash equivalents at end of period		X

Preparing a statement of cash flows

Process:

- insert the net increase or decrease in cash and cash equivalents first. This is the figure the cash flow totals to and is an easy figure to calculate. It is the difference between cash and overdraft balances and short-term investments from the prior year to the current year. You can then fill in the opening balance of cash and cash equivalents. Then move on to the rest of the cash flow.

- start with cash from operating activities – insert profit before interest and tax and add back deprecation.

- next, deal with the movements in working capital. It can be tricky to remember which way round these figures should go. The following table summarises the treatment:

	Increase	Decrease
Inventory	Outflow	Inflow
Receivables	Outflow	Inflow
Payables	Inflow	Outflow

- work your way down the rest of the cash flow dealing with the easier figures first, such as interest, dividends and tax paid and movements in borrowing.

- finally, deal with the more difficult areas (such as non-current assets and movements in share capital) where a working is required in order to find relevant cash flow figures.

CBA focus

- Cash flows are straightforward to produce if you follow a step-by-step process.
- Make sure you practise lots of questions so you are well prepared.
- Always aim to get the easy marks first and then go back and try the harder parts of the questions.

Example

The opening carrying amount of non-current assets is £490,580 and the closing balance is £567,210.

The depreciation charge for the year was £35,000.

There were disposals with a carrying amount of £43,000.

What is the cash paid for additions?

Solution

All the amounts need to be entered into the ledger account and then the missing figure is the balancing figure – in this case additions. This style of working can also be used to find tax paid.

Example

The following extract from the statement of financial position shows share capital and share premium:

Capital and reserves	20X7 £	20X6 £
Share capital	135,000	120,000
Share premium	96,000	79,000

Calculate the cash received from the issue of shares.

Solution

If there has been a share issue in the year, we must remember to look at share premium as well as share capital as it is likely that the shares have been issued at a premium.

Non-current assets (CA)

	£		£
Balance b/d	490,580	Depreciation	35,000
		Disposals	43,000
		Balance c/d	567,210
Cash additions (bal fig)	**154,630**		
	645,210		645,210

OR alternative working

Opening PPE	490,580
Depreciation	(35,000)
Disposals	(43,000)
Closing PPE	(567,210)
Purchase of PPE	**154,630**

The movement is:

Increase in share capital (135,000 – 120,000)	15,000
Increase in share premium (96,000 – 79,000)	17,000
Total cash received from share issue	32,000

Example

The opening tax payable is £6,000 and the closing tax payable is £8,000. The charge in the statement of profit or loss is £7,000 for the year.

What is the cash paid in respect of tax?

Solution:

Tax payable

	£		£
Cash paid		Balance b/d	6,000
(bal fig)	**5,000**	Tax expense	7,000
Balance c/d	8,000		
	13,000		13,000

Once all the known amounts relating to tax are entered into the ledger account, the cash paid becomes the balancing figure.

Interpretation of a statement of cash flows

Things to look for

- Operating cash flow reflects how well a business is generating cash from its day to day activities. A negative operating cash flow is not good and suggests that the business is not operating efficiently. Also look at the effect on cash flow from working capital – inventories, receivables and payables.

- Good management of working capital can mean the business uses its cash effectively. Review the cash position as well as inventory levels, receivables and payables. For example, if inventory levels have risen, is it because of increased sales or could it be obsolete inventory? Does the company have the cash to pay for an inventory increase?

- If a company has made an investment in non-current assets, then they are obviously planning for the future which is a positive move. Comment on how they have financed this investment – by finance, cash, or share issues.

- If the company has no cash, sales of non-current assets may be a 'desperate' measure to raise cash.

- Review share issues and debt movements. Often this will correlate with non-current asset purchases so you can match the asset and its related finance.

- If the company is paying a dividend, look to see if there is sufficient cash to pay it. Many companies are reluctant to reduce the dividend as it sends a negative sign to shareholders.

4

Consolidated statement of financial position

- Overview.
- Consolidated statement of financial position.

Overview

This chapter will:

- Summarise the concept of a group and the process of consolidation.

- Set out tests of control in accordance with IFRS 10.

- Summarise and illustrate the three key workings normally needed to prepare a consolidated statement of financial position in an examination task.

CBA focus

- You can expect to see a group accounting question on this paper – either a statement of financial position or statement of profit or loss.

- You must have a logical approach to consolidations by using the workings below.

Key points

- A group consists of a parent company and subsidiary companies that are controlled by the parent.

- Consolidated financial statements combine the results and net assets of the parent and subsidiaries to show the group as a single entity.

- The performance of the group as a whole is shown in the consolidated financial statements.

Control

- When a parent acquires a subsidiary it is deemed to control that subsidiary when more than 50% of the ordinary share capital has been acquired.

- IFRS 3 defines a business combination as the bringing together of separate entities (i.e. companies) into one reporting entity. In most cases, when this occurs, one entity (the parent or acquirer) acquires control of the other entities (subsidiaries or acquirees). There are different ways a business combination can be effected. In the examples in this chapter and the next chapter, one company purchases the majority of shares in another company.

- IFRS 10 allows for situations where a parent doesn't own more than 50% of share capital but exercises control in some other way. In this case, the parent should consolidate the other company as a subsidiary regardless of the % shareholding.

- Per IFRS 10, an investor controls an investee if they have power over the investee, exposure to variable returns from its involvement with the investee, and the ability to use its power over the investee to affect the amount of the investor's returns.

Consolidated statement of financial position

There are 3 workings for the group statement of financial position. Working through these in an exam question provides you with a logical process towards completing the question.

Set out your workings as follows:

Group structure

The percentage will be given in the exam question.

A

70%

B

W1 Goodwill

Cost of investment	X
less: % of share capital acquired	(X)
% of retained earnings acquired	(X)
% fair value adjustments	(X)
Goodwill	X
Impairments	(X)
Goodwill in SFP	X

W2 Non-controlling interest

NCI % share capital	X
NCI % retained earnings	X
NCI % fair value adjustment	X
NCI	X

W3 Group retained earnings

Parent (100%)	X
Subsidiary	X
(Group share of post acquisition profit)	
Impairment	(X)
	X

Further points

- To calculate goodwill, you may need to adjust the subsidiary's assets at acquisition to their fair value.
- All companies in the same group should follow the same accounting policies.
- If there are any other reserves such as revaluation surpluses, they are treated in exactly the same way as retained earnings by taking the group share of the post acquisition movement on that reserve.

CBA focus

The process to follow is:

- Read the question.
- Start with the 3 workings and insert those figures into the answer.
- Add together the assets and liabilities of parent and subsidiary line by line to finish.

Example

J Ltd purchased 60% of the shares of R Ltd for £35,000 on 1 January 20X7. The retained earnings of R Ltd at that date were £14,000 and the non-current assets had a fair value of £6,000 more than their carrying amount at that date.

The statements of financial position as at 31 December 20X7 are below.

	J Ltd £000	R Ltd £000
ASSETS		
Non-current assets	20	22
Investment in R Ltd	35	–
Current assets	18	14
Total assets	73	36
EQUITY AND LIABILITIES		
Share capital (£1 shares)	20	10
Retained earnings	39	19
Current liabilities	14	7
Total equity and liabilities	73	36

Prepare the consolidated statement of financial position at 31 December 20X7.

Solution

Group structure

J

60%

R

(W1) Goodwill	£000
Cost of investment	35
Share capital acquired (10,000 x 60%)	(6)
Retained earnings acquired (14,000 x 60%)	(8.4)
Fair value adjustments (6,000 x 60%)	(3.6)
Goodwill in SFP	17

(W2) Non-controlling interest	£000
Share capital (10,000 x 40%)	4
Retained earnings at reporting date (19,000 x 40%)	7.6
Fair value adjustment (6,000 x 40%)	2.4
	14

(W3) Group retained earnings	£000
Parent company (100%)	39
Subsidiary: Group share of post	
acquisition profit (60% × (19–14)	3
	42

J Ltd, consolidated statement of financial position as at 31 December 20X7

ASSETS	£000
Non-current assets	
Goodwill (W1)	17
Property, plant and equipment	
(20 + 22 + 6)	48
Current assets (18 + 14)	32
Total assets	97
EQUITY AND LIABILITIES	
Share capital	20
Retained earnings (W3)	42
	62
Non-controlling interest (W2)	14
Current liabilities (14 + 7)	21
Total equity and liabilities	97

5

Consolidated statement of profit or loss

- Overview.
- Consolidated statement of profit or loss.
- IFRS 10 consolidated financial statements.

Overview

This chapter will:

- Show how to prepare a consolidated statement of profit or loss, based on the same principles as those underlying a consolidated statement of financial position.

- Summarise the main points of IFRS 10 on the regulation of consolidated financial statements.

CBA focus

- As with the statement of financial position, you must have a logical approach to consolidations by using the workings below.

Key points

- The consolidated statement of profit or loss shows the group as a single entity by combining the results of the parent and subsidiaries.

- Add together the results from revenue down to and including profit after tax to show the results of the group.

- Intra-group sales and purchases between the parent and subsidiary must be removed as the statement of profit or loss shows the transactions the group as a whole has made.

- Any dividends or interest paid to the parent from the subsidiary must be excluded from the group statement of profit or loss.

Consolidated statement of profit or loss

Workings:

Group structure

The percentage will be given in the exam.

70%

W2 Revenue and cost of sales

Don't forget to remove intercompany trading from revenue and cost of sales. The whole amount of sales or purchases between the group companies must be removed.

CBA focus

When dealing with inter company trading, it is important to remember to remove THE SAME AMOUNT from both sales and from cost of sales. Failure to do this is a fundamental error of principle.

W3 Non-controlling interest

NCI share of subsidiary profit after tax   X

Example

Set out below are the draft statement of profit or loss of Perry Ltd and its subsidiary company Shale Ltd for the year ended 31 December 20X7.

On 31 December 20X5 Perry Ltd purchased 75% of the ordinary shares and 50% of the debentures of Shale Ltd. The issued share capital of Shale Ltd is 200,000 £1 ordinary shares, and it had £50,000 10% debentures outstanding on 31 December 20X7.

Shale Ltd pays its debenture interest on 31 December each year.

	Perry Ltd £	Shale Ltd £
Revenue	943,000	368,000
Cost of sales	(687,000)	(287,000)
Gross profit	256,000	81,000
Distribution costs	(76,000)	(26,000)
Admin expenses	(63,000)	(22,000)
Interest receivable – from group companies	2,500	–
Finance costs	–	(5,000)
Profit before taxation	119,500	28,000
Tax	(42,500)	(8,000)
Profit after taxation	77,000	20,000

During the year Perry Ltd sold goods to Shale Ltd for £112,000, making a profit of £35,000. These goods were all sold by Shale Ltd before the end of the year.

Prepare the consolidated statement of profit or loss for the year ended 31 December 20X7.

Solution

(W1) Group structure

Perry Ltd

75%

Shale Ltd

(W2) Revenue and cost of sales

The total revenue is £1,311,000 but the intra-group sales of £112,000 has been included as part of Perry Ltd's revenue and must be excluded, leaving £1,199,000.

Similarly, total cost of sales is £974,000 but the intra-group purchase of £112,000 has been included in cost of sales for Shale Ltd. It must be excluded, leaving £862,000.

(W3) Interest receivable

Interest receivable from group companies of £2,500 is Perry Ltd's share of the debenture interest. It must be cancelled against the finance cost in Shale Ltd to leave the net finance cost outside of the group of £2,500 (£5,000 – £2,500).

(W4) Non-controlling interests

The non-controlling interest is 25% of Shale Ltd's profit after tax figure = 25% × £20,000 = £5,000.

Perry Ltd, consolidated statement of profit or loss for the year ended 31 December 20X7

	£
Revenue (W2)	1,199,000
Cost of sales (W2)	(862,000)
Gross profit	337,000
Distribution costs (76,000 + 26,000)	(102,000)
Administrative expenses (63,000 + 22,000)	(85,000)
Finance costs (W3)	(2,500)
Profit before taxation	147,500
Tax (42,500 + 8,000)	(50,500)
Profit for the period	97,000
Attributable to:	
Equity holders of the parent	92,000
Non-controlling interests (W4)	5,000
	97,000

IFRS 10 consolidated financial statements

Key points

- A company must prepare group financial statements if it is a parent company at its year-end (i.e. it has one or more subsidiaries). The consolidated financial statements must include all of the subsidiaries of the parent.

- IFRS 10 details the consolidation procedures that we have already seen in the previous chapters, such as the requirement to eliminate inter company trading.

- IFRS 10 also states that uniform accounting policies should be used for amounts included in the group financial statements.

6

Tangible and intangible assets

- Overview.
- Measurement.
- Depreciation.
- Revaluations.
- IAS 38 Intangible Assets.
- IAS 36 Impairment of Assets.

Overview

This chapter deals with the following standards that regulate the accounting for non-current assets:

- IAS 16 Property, Plant and Equipment
- IAS 38 Intangible Assets, including research and development costs.
- IAS 36 Impairment.

CBA focus

Non-current assets are a key part of the standards for this unit. You are likely to be tested on them at some point in the exam.

Measurement

IAS 16 Property, Plant and Equipment provides guidance on non-current assets.

Key points:

- A non-current asset should be initially measured at its cost.
- Cost includes all costs that are directly attributable in bring the asset to its working condition for its intended use.
- Subsequent expenditure on an asset can be capitalised if it enhances the economic benefits of the asset, such as reconditioning an asset to provide additional years of use.

Depreciation

Definition

Depreciation represents the consumption of a non-current asset in the accounting period.

Non-current assets are used in the business to earn revenue. Charging depreciation means that the revenue earned is matched with the cost of using that asset. This applies the **accruals** concept.

The method of depreciation should be the one which gives the best estimate of the benefits of the asset consumed during the accounting period:

Benefits consumed equally in all periods	Benefits consumed more in earlier than later periods
↓	↓
Straight line	Reducing balance

Example

A non-current asset costs £10,000, has a residual value of £2,000 and an estimated life of 4 years.

What is the annual depreciation charge using the straight line method?

Solution

$$\frac{\text{Original cost} - \text{residual value}}{\text{Estimated useful life}}$$

$$\frac{£10,000 - £2,000}{4 \text{ years}}$$

This gives a depreciation charge of £2,000 each year.

Revaluations

Key points:

- Revaluation of assets is permitted but not required. If revaluations take place all assets of the same class must be revalued.

- Companies may wish to revalue assets to show a more up to date value of the assets in the business.

- If the difference between the carrying amount and the revalued amount is a gain on revaluation, it is credited to a reserve in the statement of financial position called the revaluation surplus and disclosed in the statement of changes in equity.

- If there is a loss on revaluation, it is recognised in the statement of profit or loss unless there is already a balance in the revaluation surplus relating to that asset. In that case, the loss is first taken to the revaluation surplus with any remainder in the statement of profit or loss.

- Depreciation on a revalued asset is based on the revalued amount not the cost. If the asset has increased in value this will give a higher depreciation charge. The revalued asset is depreciated over its remaining useful life from the date of revaluation.

- The depreciation charge on the revalued asset will be different to the depreciation that would have been charged based on the previous asset value. As a result of this, a transfer should be made of an amount equal to the excess depreciation from the revaluation surplus to retained earnings. The double entry for this transfer is shown below:

Dr Revaluation surplus
Cr Retained earnings

The above transfer is only required if it is company policy to make a transfer in respect of excess depreciation on revalued assets. If this is not the case then a reserves transfer is not necessary.

Example

KL Ltd own buildings which cost £350,000 on 1 January 20X4. Depreciation is charged over 50 years. On 1 January 20X6, the buildings were revalued to £480,000.

Calculate the gain on revaluation and the carrying amount of the buildings at 31 December 20X6.

Solution

We will approach this question step by step as there are a number of stages to deal with.

1. Calculate the carrying amount at the date of revaluation

	£
Cost	350,000
Depreciation to 31/12/X5	
350,000 ÷ 50 × 2 years	(14,000)
CA at 1/1/X6	336,000

2. Calculate the gain on revaluation

	£
Revalued amount	480,000
Less carrying amount	(336,000)
Gain on revaluation	144,000

DR Non-current assets – cost	
(480,000 – 350,000)	130,000
DR Accumulated depreciation	14,000
CR Revaluation surplus	144,000

3. Calculate the carrying amount at 31 December 31/12/X6

	£
Revalued amount	480,000
Depreciation to 31/12/X6	
480,000 ÷ 48 years	(10,000)
CA at 31/12/X6	470,000

> Note that once the asset has been revalued, the depreciation is calculated for the remaining useful life, in this case – 48 years.

Example

KL Ltd's accounting policy is to make the annual transfer within the SOCIE to transfer the 'excess depreciation' from revaluation surplus to retained earnings.

Calculate the excess depreciation and show the journal entries required to transfer the excess depreciation from the revaluation surplus to retained earnings at 31/12/X6.

Solution	
The transfer in the SOCIE is: £10,000 - £7,000 =	£3,000
Dr: Revaluation surplus	£3,000
Cr: Retained earnings	£3,000
CA of revaluation surplus at 31/12/X6 is £144,000 - £3,000 =	£141,000

IAS 38 Intangible Assets

Definition

IAS 38 Intangible Assets defines an intangible asset as an identifiable, non-monetary asset without physical substance.

To be identified as an intangible asset, an asset must either:

- be capable of being separated or divided from the entity and sold, transferred, licensed, rented or exchanged either individually or together with a related contract, asset or liability; or
- arise from contractual or other legal rights.

Internally generated goodwill should not be recognised as an asset as it is not a separable asset, it doesn't arise from contractual rights and it cannot be measured reliably.

Recognition and measurement

- An intangible asset shall only be recognised if:
  - it is probable that the expected future economic benefits that are attributable to the asset will flow to the entity; and
  - the cost of the asset can be measured reliably.
- An intangible asset shall initially be measured at cost.

Research and development costs

An entity must distinguish between:

- the research phase
- the development phase.

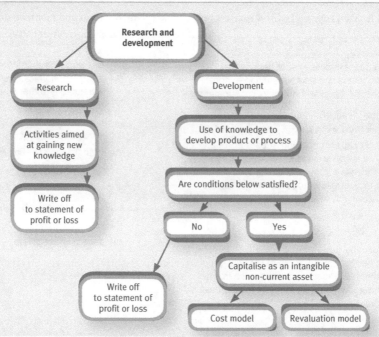

Expenditure on the **research** phase is recognised as an expense in the statement of profit or loss when it is incurred and cannot be recognised as an intangible asset.

Expenditure on the **development** phase can be recognised as an intangible asset providing the entity can demonstrate all the following conditions:

(a) technical feasibility of completing the intangible asset so it is available for use or sale.

(b) intention to complete the intangible asset and use or sell it.

(c) ability to use or sell the intangible asset.

(d) how the intangible asset will generate probable future economic benefits.

(e) availability of adequate technical, financial and other resources to complete the development and to use or sell the intangible asset.

(f) ability to measure reliably the expenditure attributable to the intangible asset during its development.

Internally generated brands, publishing titles, customer lists and similar items cannot be recognised as intangible assets.

Subsequent measurement

The cost model or revaluation model must be chosen to account for the asset once recognised.

- **Cost model:** The asset is carried at cost less any accumulated depreciation and any accumulated impairment losses.

- **Revaluation model:** The asset is carried at its revalued amount. This is its fair value at the date of revaluation less any subsequent accumulated amortisation and any subsequent impairment losses. The valuation must be reviewed regularly.

Useful life of intangible assets

Finite life

- Amortise over useful life.
- Residual value is nil unless active market for asset or agreement for purchase at end of life.

Indefinite life

- Don't amortise
- Test for impairment annually
- Review useful life annually to ensure still indefinite.

IAS 36 Impairment of Assets

Definition

Impairment is the reduction in the recoverable amount of a non-current asset below its carrying amount.

Recoverable amount is the higher of the fair value less costs to sell and value in use.

Fair value less costs to sell is the amount at which an asset could be disposed of, less any direct selling costs.

Value in use is the present value of the future cash flows arising from an asset's continued use, including those resulting from its ultimate disposal.

Indicators of impairment

The following are indicators that an asset may be impaired:

- a current period operating loss or net cash outflow from operating activities

- a significant decline in a non-current asset's market value during the period
- obsolescence or physical damage to a fixed asset
- a significant adverse change in the business or the market in which the fixed asset or goodwill is involved
- a management commitment to undertake a significant reorganisation
- a major loss of key employees, or
- a significant increase in market interest rates.

Recognising impairment losses

- Impairment losses are recognised in the statement of profit or loss, unless they arise on a previously revalued asset.
- Impairment losses on revalued assets are taken to the revaluation surplus for that asset with any remaining loss charged to the statement of profit or loss.

- After recognition of the impairment loss the depreciation charge for the asset shall be adjusted to allocate the asset's revised carrying amount over its remaining useful economic life.

Example

P Ltd owns plant and machinery that cost £150,000 on 1 January 20X2. It is depreciated over 15 years and on 1 January 20X5 it was revalued to £180,000. On 1 January 20X7, the assets were impaired and were written down to £120,000.

Calculate the impairment loss and show where it will be recorded.

Solution

1 Calculate the carrying amount at the date of revaluation

	£
Cost	150,000
Depreciation to 31/12/X4	
150,000 ÷ 15 × 3 years	(30,000)
CA at 1/1/X5	120,000

2 Calculate the gain on revaluation (1/1/X5)

	£
Revalued amount	180,000
Less carrying amount	(120,000)
Gain on revaluation	60,000

DR Non-current assets – cost	
(180,000 – 150,000)	30,000
DR Accumulated depreciation	30,000
CR Revaluation surplus	60,000

3 Calculate the carrying amount at 31 December 20X6

	£
Revalued amount	180,000
Depreciation to 31/12/X6	
180,000 ÷ 12 × 2 years	(30,000)
CV at 1/1/X6 7	150,000

4 Record the impairment on 1 January 20X7

	£
Revised value	120,000
Less CA	(150,000)
Impairment loss	30,000

As this is a revalued asset and there is sufficient revaluation surplus remaining, this impairment loss can be taken to the revaluation surplus rather than the statement of profit or loss.

DR Revaluation surplus	30,000
CR Accumulated depreciation	30,000

7

Key accounting standards

- Overview.
- IAS 2 Inventories.
- IAS 17 Leases.
- IAS 10 Events After the Reporting Period.
- IAS 37 Provisions, Contingent Liabilities and Contingent Assets.
- Other accounting standards.

Overview

This chapter deals with the main points of accounting standards not dealt with in other chapters:

- A reminder of inventory valuation principles (IAS 2).
- The treatment of leased assets in accordance with IAS 17.
- The impact on financial statements of events which take place after the reporting period (IAS 10).
- The treatment of provisions and contingencies (IAS 37).

CBA focus

One or more of the topics covered in this chapter can be expected to appear in examination tasks.

IAS 2 Inventories

Key Point

- Inventories should be stated at the **lower of cost and net realisable value**.
- Cost includes all costs of purchase, conversion and other costs incurred in bringing the inventory to its present location and condition.
- Methods of costing identical items of inventory include:
  - **Unit cost** – the actual cost of purchasing or manufacturing inventory.
  - **Weighted average cost** – calculating an average price for the inventory as it is purchased or sold.
  - **FIFO** (first in first out) – calculation that assumes the inventory held represents the latest purchases and the earlier purchases are included in sales.

IAS 17 Leases

Definition

A lease is a contract to hire out an asset between the lessor (owner) and the lessee (who holds the asset).

There are two types of lease:

Finance lease
- Lease that transfers substantially all of the risks and rewards of ownership to the lessee.

Operating lease
- A lease other than a finance lease

Typically with a finance lease, the lease term is for substantially most of the asset's life and the present value of rentals paid are substantially all of the fair value of the asset.

Land and buildings

- As land has an indefinite economic life, the lessee does not receive substantially all of the risks and rewards of ownership, so land is classified as an operating lease.

- Buildings can be treated separately to land and are classified as a finance lease if appropriate even though the related land may be an operating lease.

Accounting treatment

1   Assets held under finance leases are capitalised at the fair value of the leased asset or the present value of the minimum lease payments if lower.

　　DR Non-current assets

　　　　CR Leasing obligation

2   Depreciation is charged on the leased asset over the lower of the lease term and the asset's useful economic life.

3   Interest is charged on the outstanding leasing obligation and is shown as an expense in the statement of profit or loss.

DR Interest expense
    CR Leasing obligation

Example

A lessee enters into a lease on 1 January 20X6 for an item of plant with a life of four years. The following details are relevant:

Fair value of asset   £25,000

Residual value   Nil after four years

Lease terms £7,500 pa in advance for four years, the first rental payable on 1 Jan X6.

The interest rate implicit in the lease is 13.7%.

Calculate the interest charge and the closing obligation over the period of the lease.

Solution

The easiest way to deal with leases is to put the information in a table and work through year by year. That way you can calculate the interest and the obligation in the same working.

The interest column shows the interest charge for each year. Notice how it reduces as the obligation is reducing.

The balance c/fwd column shows the obligation for the lease at the end of each year. This represents the total amount still owed.

Operating leases

With an operating lease there is no suggestion that the risks and rewards of ownership are transferred from the lessor to the lessee. The asset is not capitalised, instead the rentals paid are charged to the statement of profit or loss on a straight-line basis over the lease term.

	Balance b/fwd	Payment	Amount borrowed	Interest 13.7%	Balance c/fwd
Year ended 31 Dec X6	25,000	(7,500)	17,500	2,398	19,898
Year ended 31 Dec X7	19,898	(7,500)	12,398	1,698	14,096
Year ended 31 Dec X8	14,096	(7,500)	6,596	904	7,500
Year ended 31 Dec X9	7,500	(7,500)	0		

IAS 10 Events After the Reporting Period

Definition

- **Events after the reporting period** are those events, favourable and unfavourable, that occur between the end of the reporting period and the date when the financial statements are authorised for issue.

- **Adjusting events** are events after the reporting period are those that provide evidence of conditions that existed at the end of the reporting period.

- **Non-adjusting events** are events after the reporting period that are indicative of conditions that arose after the end of the reporting period.

Accounting treatment:

- **Adjusting events** affect the amounts stated in the financial statements so they must be **adjusted**.

- **Non-adjusting events** do not concern the position at the end of the reporting period so the financial statements are not adjusted. If the event is material then the nature and its financial effect must be **disclosed**.

Examples of adjusting events:

- The sale of inventory after the year-end date that gives evidence about the inventory's net realisable value at the end of the reporting period.

- The bankruptcy of a customer after the reporting period that confirms that an allowance is required against a receivable balance at the end of the reporting period.

- The discovery of fraud or errors that show that the financial statements are incorrect.

- The settlement after the reporting period of a court case that confirms that the entity had a present obligation at the end of the reporting period. This would require a provision to be recognised in the financial statements (or an existing provision to be adjusted).

Examples of non-adjusting events that would require disclosure:

- A major business combination after the reporting period or disposing of a major subsidiary.
- Announcing a plan to discontinue an operation.
- Major purchases and disposals of assets.
- Destruction of a major production plant by a fire after the reporting period.
- Announcing or commencing a major restructuring.

- Abnormally large changes after the end of the reporting period in asset prices or foreign exchange rates.

Dividends:

- Ordinary dividends declared **after** the reporting period are **not recognised** as liabilities at the statement of financial position.
- This is consistent with IAS 37 and the definition of a liability in the Framework.

IAS 37 Provisions, Contingent Liabilities and Contingent Assets

Definition

- A **provision** is a liability of uncertain timing or amount.
- A **liability** is a present obligation arising from past events
- An **obligating event** is an event that creates a legal or constructive obligation
- **Constructive obligation** – this arises from an entity's past actions, where there is a pattern of past practice that indicates they will behave in a certain way e.g. remedy environmental damage even if not legally required.
- IAS 37 prohibits provisions for future **operating losses** - they are avoidable

CBA focus

In an exam task, ask yourself if the expenditure can be avoided.

If it can, there is no obligation and the provision should not be recognised.

Provisions

Recognition

Recognise when:
- an entity has a present obligation (legal or constructive) as a result of a past event,
- it is probable that a transfer of economic benefits will be required to settle the obligation, and
- a reliable estimate can be made of the amount of the obligation.

Measurement

The amount recognised:
- as a provision should be the best estimate of the expenditure required to settle the present obligation at the statement of financial position date.
- Where the time value of money is material, the provision should be discounted to present value.

Contingent assets and liabilities

- A **contingent liability** is a possible obligation arising from past events whose existence will only be confirmed on the occurrence of uncertain future events outside of the entity's control.

- A **contingent asset** is a **possible** asset that arises from past events and whose existence will only be confirmed on the occurrence of uncertain future events outside of the entity's control.

Contingent liabilities should not be recognised. They should be **disclosed** unless the possibility of a transfer of economic benefits is remote.

Contingent assets should not be recognised. If the possibility of an inflow of economic benefits is **probable** they should be **disclosed**.

Other accounting standards

IAS 18 Revenue

- Revenue is recognised when it is probable that future economic benefits will flow to the entity.
- Revenue from the sale of goods shall be recognised when:
  - entity has transferred the risk and rewards of ownership to the buyer
  - entity does not manage or control the goods sold
  - revenue and costs can be reliably measured
  - probable that economic benefits will flow to the entity
- To recognise revenue from the provision of services it must be possible to measure the stage of completion of the transaction and the costs to complete.

IAS 12 Income Taxes

- The tax charge in the statement of profit or loss comprises of the:
  - tax expense on profits for the period.
  - under/overprovision for previous year.
- Disclosure
  - The tax charge must be shown on the face of the statement of profit or loss.

Recommended additional reading on accounting standards

A student's guide to International Financial Reporting Standards by Clare Finch

ISBN 978 1 84710 708 4

8

Interpretation of financial statements

- Overview.
- Uses of ratios.
- Key ratios.
- Limitations of ratio analysis.

Overview

This chapter deals with the topics involved in 'interpretation of accounts'. This includes:

- the uses of accounting ratios.
- the calculation and meaning of accounting ratios.
- the limitations of ratio analysis.

Uses of ratios

Key Point

- Ratio analysis is a means of interpreting financial statements.

- Users will review the financial statements and make decisions based on the information given. Ratios are calculated and compared with:

  - the performance of the business in previous years

  - the budgeted or planned performance in the current year

  - the performance of similar businesses.

- Ratios can assist in pointing the user of the financial statements to areas where the company may be performing particularly well or badly. They do not in themselves provide an answer but they can help in indicating the right direction for further investigation.

- The types of ratio to use will depend on the user of the information. For example, banks and lenders will be interested in liquidity ratios; management will be interested in profitability ratios.
- Ratios fall into several categories:
  - profitability ratios
  - liquidity and working capital ratios
  - investor ratios.

Key ratios

Ratios are important tools to assist in the interpretation of financial statements. You must learn these ratios and be able to calculate and interpret them as an exam task will require you to do both.

Profitability ratios

- **Return on capital employed (ROCE) =**

$$\frac{\text{Profit from operations}}{\text{Total equity + Non-current liabilities}} \times 100$$

ROCE is very important as it shows the profit generated from the capital employed in the business. If ROCE has increased it is due to either increases in profitability and/or increases in asset utilisation.

- **Return on shareholder's funds =**

$$\frac{\text{Profit after tax}}{\text{Total equity}} \times 100$$

- **Gross profit percentage =**

$$\frac{\text{Gross profit}}{\text{Revenue}} \times 100$$

This shows the profit made on revenue before accounting for overhead costs. An increase or decrease may be due to a change in the sales mix, changes in costs or selling prices.

- **Expense/Revenue percentage**

$$\frac{\text{Specified expense}}{\text{Revenue}} \times 100$$

This can apply to any expense

- **Operating profit percentage =**

$$\frac{\text{Profit from operations}}{\text{Revenue}} \times 100$$

This shows the profitability after taking into account expenses. A change may be due to changes in costs. You might expect an increase if sales have increased, but must watch out for costs that are rising above any sales increase as it may be that costs are not being controlled.

Liquidity

- **The current ratio =**

$$\frac{\text{Current assets}}{\text{Current liabilities}}$$

- **The quick ratio =** *(Acid Test)*

$$\frac{\text{Current assets} - \text{inventory}}{\text{Current liabilities}}$$

These two ratios show whether a business can cover its current liabilities from current assets. The quick ratio removes inventory as this is the least liquid current asset. If the ratio is too low, it may suggest the business will have trouble paying current liabilities and if the ratio is too high it may suggest that working capital is not being used efficiently.

This ratio can vary greatly from industry to industry.

Chapter 8

Use of resources

- **Inventory turnover =**

$$\frac{\text{Cost of sales}}{\text{Inventories}}$$

  Companies have to strike a balance between being able to satisfy customers' requirements from inventory and the cost of having too much capital tied up in inventory.

- **Inventory holding period =**

$$\frac{\text{Inventories}}{\text{Cost of sales}} \times 365 \text{ days}$$

  This shows how long inventory is being held before use.

- **Asset turnover (net assets) =**

$$\frac{\text{Revenue}}{\text{Total assets - current liabilities}}$$

- **Trade receivables collection period =**

$$\frac{\text{Trade receivables}}{\text{Revenue}} \times 365 \text{ days}$$

If the receivables collection period becomes too high, the business may suffer from poor cash flow. Retail companies do not usually have receivables so this ratio would be irrelevant for those companies.

- **Trade payables payment period =**

$$\frac{\text{Trade payables}}{\text{Cost of sales}} \times 365 \text{ days}$$

  Extending the payables payment period can be a cheap source of finance but companies run the risk of upsetting suppliers and not being offered credit in the future.

- **Working Capital Cycle =**
  Inventory days + Receivables days – Payables days.

- **Asset turnover (non-current assets) =**

$$\frac{\text{Revenue}}{\text{non-current assets}}$$

Financial position

- **Interest cover =**

  $$\frac{\text{Profit from operations}}{\text{Finance costs}}$$

  This shows how many times the interest charge can be paid out of the current profits. It is a measure of security - the higher the ratio, the more secure the interest payment.

- **Gearing =**

  $$\frac{\text{Non-current liabilities}}{\text{Total equity + Non-current liabilities}} \times 100$$

  This ratio shows the proportion of debt to total finance in the business (equity plus debt). The higher the gearing ratio, the riskier a company is seen to be as debt interest must be paid out before dividends.

Limitations of ratio analysis

- Ratios do not provide answers; they merely highlight significant features or trends in the financial statements. They usually highlight areas that need further investigation.

- Be mindful of seasonal trade as accounting year-ends are often just after the seasonal trend is over when the business is at its best.

- Watch out for window dressing in the financial statements such as collecting receivables just before the year-end in order to show a larger cash balance and lower receivables than is normal.

- Accounting ratios are based on accounting information and are only as accurate as that underlying accounting information.

- If comparisons are to be made they must be with companies with a similar trade, otherwise the pattern of ratios will be different and the comparisons meaningless.

Index

A

C

E

F

G

I